S0-AQJ-440

Dear Parents and Educators,

Welcome to Penguin Young Readers! As parents and educators, you know that each child develops at their own pace—in terms of speech, critical thinking, and, of course, reading. Penguin Young Readers recognizes this fact. As a result, each Penguin Young Readers book is assigned a traditional easy-to-read level (1–4) as well as an F&P Text Level (A–R). Both of these systems will help you choose the right book for your child. Please refer to the back of each book for specific leveling information. Penguin Young Readers features esteemed authors and illustrators, stories about favorite characters, fascinating nonfiction, and more!

Here Comes the Rain!
Can Animals Predict the Weather?

LEVEL **4**

F&P TEXT LEVEL **Q**

This book is perfect for a **Fluent Reader** who:
- can read the text quickly with minimal effort;
- has good comprehension skills;
- can self-correct (can recognize when something doesn't sound right); and
- can read aloud smoothly and with expression.

Here are some **activities** you can do during and after reading this book:
- Comprehension: After reading this book, answer the following questions:
  - When did Groundhog Day begin?
  - What is one reason why dogs may bark before a storm?
  - How do ants prepare for a rainstorm?
  - At what temperature do crickets begin to chirp?
  - What type of animal is a woolly bear?
- Creative Writing: Pretend you live on a farm and you see a dog start barking because it senses an earthquake coming. Write a paragraph about what you would do in that situation and what you observe around you.

Remember, sharing the love of reading with a child is the best gift you can give!

*This book has been officially leveled by using the F&P Text Level Gradient™ leveling system.

For author Peter Wohlleben, whose books about nature have helped me to further understand and more fully appreciate the interconnectedness of all living things—GLC

PENGUIN YOUNG READERS
An imprint of Penguin Random House LLC, New York

First published in the United States of America by Penguin Young Readers,
an imprint of Penguin Random House LLC, New York, 2022

Text copyright © 2022 by Ginjer L. Clarke

Photo credits: used throughout: (photo frames) happyfoto/E+/Getty Images, Tolga TEZCAN/ E+/Getty Images; cover, 3: RimenPix/iStock/Getty Images; 4–5: MicheleVacchiano/iStock/Getty Images; 6: Ugur Aydedim/iStock/Getty Images; 7: Brett Carlsen/Getty Images News/Getty Images; 8: Alexander Turnbull Library, Wellington, New Zealand (Ref: Eph-B-FARM-1885-01); 9: Simon J Beer/ iStock/Getty Images; 10: eurotravel/iStock/Getty Images; 11: nedomacki/iStock/Getty Images; 12: Oleg Minitskiy/iStock/Getty Images; 13: mynewturtle/iStock/Getty Images; 14: ps50ace/iStock/Getty Images; 15: FionaAyerst/iStock/Getty Images; 16: Jupiterimages/PHOTOS.com>>/Getty Images; 16–17: (background) Meindert van der Haven/iStock/Getty Images; 18: HunterBliss/iStock/Getty Images; 18–19: (background) ollinka/iStock/Getty Images; 20: paule858/iStock/Getty Images; 21: Heather Broccard-Bell/iStock/Getty Images; 22: BruceBlock/iStock/Getty Images; 23: ErikAgar/iStock/ Getty Images; 24: amnat jomjun/iStock/Getty Images; 25: CreativeNature_nl/iStock/Getty Images; 26–27: (background) ElementalImaging/E+/Getty Images; 27: Gerald Corsi/iStock/Getty Images; 28: mauribo/E+/Getty Images; 29: (top) SteveMcsweeny/iStock/Getty Images, (bottom) Ian Dyball/ iStock/Getty Images; 30: EzumeImages/iStock/Getty Images; 31: sdominick/iStock/Getty Images; 32: SallyNewcomb/iStock/Getty Images; 33: MirasWonderland/iStock/Getty Images; 34: kokodrill/iStock/ Getty Images; 35: Ben185/iStock/Getty Images; 36: JasonOndreicka/iStock/Getty Images; 37: (front) lenaxf/iStock/Getty Images, (middle) Richard Par/iStock/Getty Images, (back) susandaniels/iStock/ Getty Images; 38: MikeLane45/iStock/Getty Images; 39: GOLFX/iStock/Getty Images; 40: Xieyouding/ iStock/Getty Images; 41: Dwi Yulianto/iStock/Getty Images; 42: davemhuntphotography/iStock/Getty Images; 43: Siempreverde22/iStock/Getty Images; 44: Gerard Koudenburg/iStock/Getty Images; 45: (top) mikedabell/iStock/Getty Images, (bottom) MatusDuda/iStock/Getty Images; 46: tommaso79/ iStock/Getty Images; 47: Kim Steele/Photodisc/Getty Images; 48: FluxFactory/E+/Getty Images

Penguin supports copyright. Copyright fuels creativity, encourages diverse voices, promotes free speech, and creates a vibrant culture. Thank you for buying an authorized edition of this book and for complying with copyright laws by not reproducing, scanning, or distributing any part of it in any form without permission. You are supporting writers and allowing Penguin to continue to publish books for every reader.

Visit us online at penguinrandomhouse.com.

Library of Congress Cataloging-in-Publication Data is available.

Manufactured in China

ISBN 9780593383995 (pbk)   10 9 8 7 6 5 4 3 2 1 WKT
ISBN 9780593384008 (hc)   10 9 8 7 6 5 4 3 2 1 WKT

PENGUIN YOUNG READERS

LEVEL
FLUENT
READER
4

HERE COMES THE RAIN!

CAN ANIMALS PREDICT THE WEATHER?

by Ginjer L. Clarke

What Does the Groundhog Say?

It is February 2, Groundhog Day. America's most famous weather-predicting animal is ready for his big day. Phil the groundhog lives in Punxsutawney, Pennsylvania (say: PUNK-suh-taw-nee). *Yawn!* He wakes up from his long winter nap.

Punxsutawney Phil does not see his shadow when it is cloudy. Legend says that means spring will come soon. Yay! Phil *would* see his shadow if it was sunny. Then legend says winter would last longer. How did a groundhog's predictions become so special?

Groundhog Day began in 1887 in the United States. Similar traditions go back hundreds of years. People in Germany first used shadows from lit candles to predict spring. They celebrated Candlemas Day on February 2. Then they started watching hedgehogs' shadows instead of using candles. Weird!

Later, many Germans moved to
Pennsylvania. The groundhog became
their official weather predictor.
Many groundhogs have been called
Punxsutawney Phil since Groundhog Day
was started.

ROBERT WILKIN & Co's

NEW ZEALAND FARMERS

ALMANAC

18 85

NOVA ZEALANDIA

FERTILIS

TELLUS

FRUGUM PECORISQUE

·NINTH·YEAR·OF·ISSUE·

WHITCOMBE & TOMBS, LIMITED, CHRISTCHURCH. Lith.

Phil the groundhog wakes up to his inner alarm clock. It is unlikely that he can truly predict how long winter will last. But some animals *do* know when changes in weather are coming.

Weather is especially important to farmers. They watch animal behavior to help understand the weather. A book called the *Farmer's Almanac*, first written two hundred years ago, turned many animal reactions into sayings. Farmers still use these sayings to help them.

Let's find out which animals can predict weather—and how they do it!

Ready for Rain

One of the most famous *Farmer's Almanac* sayings is: "If sheep gather in a huddle, tomorrow will have a puddle." This means the sheep crowd together to keep warm and dry because they know rain is coming.

Another old farmers' saying is that when cows sense rain, they lie down to save a dry spot for later.

Scientists are not sure if this is true. But both sheep and cows can smell changes in the air and feel the winds right before a storm. They stay close to home when they sense danger. Good plan!

Run-run-run! Small songbirds called
chaffinches make this warning call when
it looks like rain. They say *chip-chip-chip*
instead when it is sunny. Most birds get
quiet before a storm and then sing again
after it passes.

Croak! Croak! Frogs also get noisier before it rains. They are not warning one another, though. The male frogs are calling to the females to mate. After rain is the best time for female frogs to lay their eggs in water.

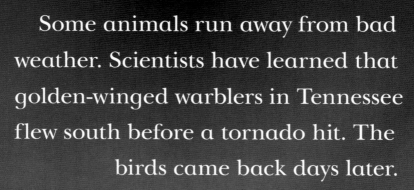

Some animals run away from bad weather. Scientists have learned that golden-winged warblers in Tennessee flew south before a tornado hit. The birds came back days later. They believe the warblers can hear low sounds that humans cannot. These birds hear storms from far away. Amazing!

Another animal with good senses is a surprising one—sharks! Experts say some types of sharks can feel changes underwater that tell the sharks when hurricanes are coming. *Whoosh!* They dive deeper to wait out the danger.

Some animals have such sensitive hearing that a drop in air pressure may hurt their ears. Air pressure is related to the weight of air. Low air pressure happens when water builds up in clouds before a storm.

Howl! Wolves may howl more before a rainstorm, possibly because of the pain from low air pressure.

Woof! Woof! Pet dogs also bark more before a storm. They feel changes in air pressure, rumbles from thunder, and electricity from lightning, even from far away. This can also make dogs pace, scratch, or hide.

Honeybees can also feel air pressure and temperature changes. *Buzz! Buzz!* They stop flying around flower beds and return to their hives when they sense rain or wind.

Some scientists studied honeybees. They learned that the bees seem to know rain is coming a full day ahead. The bees work longer than usual when rain is on the way. They are gathering extra food—pollen from flowers. They are busy bees!

19

Ants work hard when they know rain is coming, too. They build up walls around their nests, called anthills, to protect them from heavy rain. Sometimes they even cover the hole at the top of their anthill to keep out the rain.

Thrips are tiny insects that are well known for predicting rain. This gives them the nicknames "storm bugs" or "thunderflies." *Zoom!* Thrips often swarm in the thousands right before a storm. This probably happens because they fly best in air that is humid, or water filled.

Sunnier Days Ahead

Another insect swarm tells us when sunshine, not rain, is headed our way. The *Farmer's Almanac* says, "When ladybugs swarm, expect a day that's warm." You can spot these lucky little beetles gathering in groups on warm days, especially in fall. Nice!

Crane flies look like mosquitoes, but they do not bite people. They do tell us when it is getting warmer, though! Like ladybugs, they swarm once the temperature is above freezing.

Want to know if today is going to be warm? Just count cricket chirps! Crickets cannot chirp until it is at least 55 degrees Fahrenheit. Crickets chirp by rubbing their wings together. They chirp faster as they get warmer.

One scientist figured out that you can find the temperature by counting the number of cricket chirps for 14 seconds and then adding 40. This is called using a cricket thermometer. Try it!

25

Some birds can sense warmer weather, too. They migrate, or fly long distances from one place to another, as the seasons change. They usually fly south in the fall to a warmer place and return north in the spring. How do they know when to go?

Cranes start flying north as soon as they feel warming temperatures. Their arrival means that spring is coming soon. Migrating birds, not groundhogs, are the real predictors of spring!

Seagulls also tell us when the weather will stay sunny. *Swoop!* They glide over the ocean and dive for fish. Rain is likely coming when they fly over land for safety.

Another bird saying is: "Hawks flying high means a clear sky; when they fly low, prepare for a blow." This means it will be a sunny day if you see hawks soaring up high. They fly lower when the air pressure of a storm makes it harder for them to fly high.

Snow Days on the Way

Some people try to predict the start of spring on Groundhog Day. Others try to predict what winter will bring. The Woollybear Festival began in Vermilion, Ohio, in October 1973. But what is a woolly bear? And what does it know about winter?

A woolly bear is *not* a type of bear. It is a fuzzy caterpillar! This caterpillar's body has black and brown bands. The saying is that winter will be snowier when the woolly bear's black bands are longer.

The bands are probably related to what the caterpillars eat in the summer, not to the coming winter. But the woolly bear inspired the fun festival, which is still held in a few US and Canadian towns.

Squirrels are also believed to help us predict winter. And it is interesting to watch their funny behaviors.

Some people say winter will be colder if squirrels build nests higher in trees. But their nests really tell us about the current weather, not what the future weather will be.

Another idea is that squirrels work hard to gather more food for a snowy winter. *Skitter, scatter!* But hungry squirrels probably just collect more nuts in years when the trees grow more, so they seem busy.

Moles collect food for winter, too. *Scritch, scratch!* They dig in the dirt and gather earthworms. Then they store the worms to eat throughout winter. Winter is supposed to be very cold if the moles save a lot of worms.

Some people also believe that winter will be hard when moles dig their tunnels deep in the ground. But the moles dig deep to keep their tunnels from flooding when snow melts. What clever critters!

Some animals, such as mice, snakes, and spiders, try to hide inside people's houses when the weather outside turns cold. Black widow spiders really dislike the cold. Yikes!

If you suddenly see spiders in your house, they are probably seeking warmth—and warning you that winter is coming. Just be careful of dark corners, and you will be fine. Most spiders hide from people as much as the cold.

Earthquake!

Rumble, rumble! People can feel an earthquake once it starts shaking the ground. But we cannot always predict where or when an earthquake will hit. Some animals can, though!

A Roman author wrote thousands of years ago about a big earthquake. He said that many animals fled a city in Greece five days before the earthquake started. Rats, weasels, snakes, and centipedes were seen coming out of the ground and leaving the city for safety. Wow!

Scientists today agree that snakes and other animals living underground can feel the first rumbles of an earthquake. They are studying whether the animals feel the ground moving or sense electrical changes in the air.

In 1975, snakes left their winter dens to escape a massive earthquake that struck a city in China. *Hiss! Hiss!* This unusual behavior actually helped warn people to get out of the city.

Other animals have been seen reacting in strange ways, too. In 2009, a large group of toads left their lake in Italy days before an earthquake. *Hop! Hop!* A change in the water may have alerted them to danger.

Whoop! Whoop! In 2011, lemurs at the National Zoo in Washington, DC, all started calling loudly. They seemed to know that an earthquake was coming about 15 minutes before the ground started shaking.

All the animals on a farm get upset if a few animals start behaving strangely. This sometimes happens right before an earthquake.

First, the dogs sense the earthquake and bark. Then the cows hear the barking and rush down a hill. This makes the sheep run around. *Squawk! Squawk!* The chickens flap and flutter. *Flip, flop!* Even fish in a pond swim wildly.

These scared animals might not know
what an earthquake is, but they do sense
danger!

People and Weather

Some people feel pain from low air pressure like wolves and dogs do. They often get headaches the day before a storm arrives. Ouch!

But most people cannot predict the weather without fancy machines. A meteorologist (say: ME-tee-oh-RAH-la-jist) works very hard to help people know what weather to expect. Animals do not need machines, though!

Will it be sunny, rainy, or snowy tomorrow? Watch the animals around you, because they may know what weather is coming. No matter what, have fun playing outside!